Contents

- Building a customer base and generating revenue

Chapter 6: Growing the Business

- Scaling the business and expanding operations
- Hiring employees and building a team
- Developing partnerships and collaborations

Chapter 7: Managing Risks and Challenges

- Identifying and mitigating risks
- Overcoming obstacles and challenges
- Dealing with failure and pivoting when necessary

Chapter 8: Sustaining Success

- Maintaining a competitive edge
- Innovating and adapting to changing market conditions
- Building a legacy and giving back to the community

Conclusion:

- The entrepreneurial journey is a dynamic and challenging process, but it can also be rewarding and fulfilling.
- Encouragement to act and pursue your entrepreneurial dreams.

Introduction

Entrepreneurship is the process of creating or starting a new business or venture with the aim of generating profit and value for customers and stakeholders. At least that is the dictionary definition. I prefer to say we are the dreamers and risk-takers who dare leap into the unknown and change the world around us.

Entrepreneurs are individuals who are willing to take risks, innovate, and seize opportunities to create something new and valuable.

Entrepreneurship is an important driver of economic growth and job creation, as well as a catalyst for social and environmental change. Entrepreneurs can identify and solve problems, disrupt existing industries, and create new markets and opportunities.

To be a successful entrepreneur, one needs to have an entrepreneurial mindset, which involves a combination of creativity, resilience, adaptability, and a willingness to learn and act. This mindset is essential for navigating the challenges and uncertainties of the entrepreneurial journey.

The purpose of this book is to provide a comprehensive guide to the entrepreneurial process, from generating ideas to sustaining success. It is designed to help aspiring entrepreneurs and early-stage startups navigate the complex and dynamic landscape of entrepreneurship and develop the skills, knowledge, and mindset needed to succeed.

The book is structured in a logical and sequential manner, with each chapter covering a different aspect of the entrepreneurial process. It provides practical advice, tools, and examples to help readers apply the concepts and principles to their own businesses or ventures.

Whether you are an aspiring entrepreneur, a startup founder, or a business owner looking to innovate and grow, this book will provide you with the insights and guidance you need to take your ideas from conception to successful implementation.

The book is divided into eight chapters, each covering a critical stage of the entrepreneurial process.

In the first chapter, we will explore techniques for generating ideas and identifying opportunities in the market. This will be followed by a chapter on conducting market research to understand customer needs and preferences and analyzing competitors and market trends.

Chapter three will focus on building a business plan, which is a crucial tool for outlining the company's strategy, marketing plan, and financial projections. The fourth chapter will cover sources of funding for the business, including loans, grants, and investments, as well as strategies for pitching to investors and managing finances.

Chapter five will delve into the process of launching the business, including preparing for launch day, building a brand, and generating revenue. Chapter six will cover strategies for scaling the business, including hiring employees, developing partnerships, and expanding operations.

In the seventh chapter, we will discuss strategies for managing risks and overcoming obstacles, as well as dealing with failure and pivoting when necessary. Finally, in chapter eight, we will explore ways to sustain success over the long term, including maintaining a competitive edge, innovating, and giving back to the community.

Chapter 1: Generating Ideas

"Creativity is not about waiting for the perfect idea, it's about cultivating a garden of ideas and nurturing them to fruition."

Generating ideas is the first and perhaps the most critical step in the entrepreneurial process. It requires creativity, curiosity, and a deep understanding of the market and customer needs. In this chapter, we will explore techniques for generating ideas, evaluating, and selecting the best ideas, and identifying opportunities in the market.

Idea Generation Techniques

There are several techniques that can be used to generate new business ideas. One of the most popular is brainstorming, which involves generating as many ideas as possible without evaluating or judging them. This technique encourages creativity and free thinking and can lead to unexpected and innovative ideas.

One technique for generating ideas is brainstorming. To try this technique, follow these steps:

1. Gather a group of people who are familiar with the problem or opportunity you are trying to address.

2. Set a time limit of about 10-15 minutes for the brainstorming session.

3. Start by stating the problem or opportunity clearly and concisely.

4. Encourage everyone to share their ideas, no matter how seemingly silly or unconventional they may be.

5. Build on each other's ideas and avoid criticizing or dismissing any ideas at this stage.

6. Use prompts or questions to spark new ideas, such as "What if we could do the opposite of what everyone else is doing?" or "How can we make this more efficient?"

7. After the time limit is up, review the list of ideas and choose the most promising ones to further evaluate and develop.

For example, if the problem is "How can we improve the online shopping experience for customers?" during a brainstorming session, some ideas that may be generated could include:

- Implementing a virtual try-on feature for clothing and accessories

- Offering personalized recommendations based on customers' past purchases and browsing history

- Adding a chatbot for customer support and assistance

- Offering faster and more flexible shipping and delivery options

- Creating a loyalty program with exclusive perks and rewards

Another technique is called mind mapping, which involves creating a visual representation of ideas and their relationships. This technique can help to organize and prioritize ideas and identify areas where more research is needed.

Let's say you want to start a new restaurant, and you're brainstorming ideas for the menu. You start with the central idea "restaurant menu" and branch out with subtopics like "appetizers," "entrees," "drinks," and "desserts." Under each subtopic, you can then generate more specific ideas. For example, under "appetizers," you might write down "bruschetta," "fried calamari," and "spinach dip."

As you continue to brainstorm, you can keep adding new subtopics and ideas, and connect them in a way that makes sense to you. This can help you organize your thoughts and come up with new ideas you might not have considered otherwise.

Other techniques include role-playing, where individuals imagine themselves in different scenarios and generate ideas based on those scenarios, and observation, where entrepreneurs observe customer behavior and identify unmet needs or pain points.

Let's say you're a team of entrepreneurs trying to come up with ideas for a new mobile app. You can use role-playing to generate ideas by assigning each team member a different role to play. For example, one team member could pretend to be a user with specific needs or problems that they want the app to solve. Another team member could play the role of a developer, thinking about the technical aspects of building the app. Yet another team member could play the role of a marketer, considering how to promote the app and generate user interest.

Through role-playing, each team member can bring a unique perspective to the idea generation process and explore different angles for the app. The team can then collaborate to combine and refine the ideas generated through the role-playing exercise.

Evaluating and Selecting Ideas

Once you have generated a list of potential ideas, the next step is to evaluate and select the best ones. This involves considering several factors, such as the feasibility of the idea, the potential market size, and the competition.

One tool that can be used to evaluate ideas is the SWOT analysis, which stands for strengths, weaknesses, opportunities, and threats. This analysis helps to identify the strengths and weaknesses of the idea and the opportunities and threats in the market.

here's an example of a SWOT analysis for a startup idea in the food delivery industry:

Strengths:

- Innovative technology to make the ordering process easier and more efficient
- Unique delivery model that sets us apart from competitors

- Strong partnerships with local restaurants
- Experienced management team with a proven track record of success

Weaknesses:

- Limited brand recognition in a crowded market
- Dependence on external food delivery partners for the actual delivery
- Potential challenges in hiring and retaining quality drivers
- Uncertainty around how customers will respond to the new delivery model

Opportunities:

- Growing demand for food delivery services, particularly during the pandemic
- Ability to expand into new geographic markets and partner with more restaurants
- Diversification of service offerings, such as adding grocery delivery or meal kits

Threats:

- Intense competition in the food delivery market
- Changes in customer preferences or behaviors due to the pandemic or other external factors
- Regulatory changes that could impact our business model
- Economic downturn or recession affecting consumer spending habits

Another tool is the Lean Canvas, which is a one-page business plan that helps to outline the key components of the business idea, such as the problem it solves, the target customer, and the revenue streams.

Identifying Opportunities in the Market

To identify opportunities in the market, entrepreneurs need to understand the needs and preferences of their target customers, as well as the trends and dynamics of the market. This involves conducting market research and analyzing data to identify gaps and unmet needs.

One useful approach is to identify trends in the market, such as changes in customer behavior or new technologies, and use these trends as a basis for generating new business ideas.

One trend in the market is the growing demand for plant-based food options. This trend is driven by a variety of factors, including health concerns, environmental sustainability, and animal welfare. One potential business idea based on this trend is to create a meal delivery service that specializes in vegan and vegetarian cuisine. This service could offer a variety of meal plans that cater to different dietary needs and preferences and could also include options for people with food allergies or sensitivities. By focusing on the plant-based food trend, this business could tap into a growing market and meet the needs of consumers who are looking for healthy, sustainable, and ethical food options.

Another approach is to identify unmet needs in the market and develop solutions to address these needs. One unmet need in the market is the lack of convenient and affordable transportation options for people living in urban areas. This need is particularly acute for people who live in areas that are not well-served by public transportation, or who need to travel outside of regular operating hours. To address this need, an entrepreneur could develop a ride-sharing platform that connects drivers with passengers who are looking for a ride. This platform could operate on a flexible schedule, allowing passengers to request rides at any time of day or night, and could also offer affordable pricing options to make it accessible to a wide range of users. By addressing the unmet need for convenient and affordable transportation, this platform could fill a gap in the market and provide value to its users.

Ultimately, the key to generating successful business ideas is to stay curious, open-minded, and proactive in identifying opportunities in the market. By using a combination of idea generation techniques, evaluation tools, and market research, entrepreneurs can identify and select the best ideas and create value for their customers and stakeholders.

Developing a successful business idea is not just about generating a great idea. It's also about having a deep understanding of the market and the customers that you are trying to serve. In this section, we'll explore some ways that entrepreneurs can gather information and identify opportunities in the market.

One of the most effective ways to gather information about the market is through customer interviews. These interviews can help entrepreneurs to identify pain points and unmet needs, as well as to understand how customers are currently addressing those needs. By listening to customers and gathering their feedback, entrepreneurs can gain valuable insights that can be used to refine and improve their business ideas.

Another useful tool is market analysis. This involves gathering data about the size and characteristics of the market, as well as the key players and trends. Market analysis can help entrepreneurs to identify opportunities for growth, as well as potential threats or challenges.

Suppose you are interested in starting a food delivery business in a certain city. You would begin by conducting a market analysis to determine if there is demand for such a service, who your competitors are, and how you could differentiate your business.

First, you would look at demographic data to determine if there is a large enough target market in the area. You might find that there are a lot of young professionals who are too busy to cook and prefer to order food online.

Next, you would research your competitors to see how they are currently serving this market. You might find that there are a few large food delivery services that dominate the market, but also some smaller, niche players.

Finally, you would consider how you could differentiate your business from the competition. For example, you might offer a wider variety of cuisine options or specialize in healthy, organic food. You might also offer faster delivery times or lower prices.

Overall, the market analysis would help you determine whether there is a viable opportunity for your food delivery business in that city, and what steps you would need to take to make it successful.

Entrepreneurs can also learn a lot by studying successful businesses in their industry. By understanding what has worked for other businesses, entrepreneurs can gain valuable insights that they can apply to their own business ideas.

Finally, entrepreneurs should always be looking for opportunities to innovate and differentiate themselves from the competition. This can involve exploring new technologies, experimenting with new business models, or finding creative ways to deliver value to customers.

Here's an example of how a new coffee shop could differentiate themselves from the competition:

The new coffee shop could differentiate itself from the competition by offering unique and high-quality coffee blends that are not available at other coffee shops. They could also focus on creating a welcoming and cozy atmosphere in the shop, with comfortable seating, artwork on the walls, and live music or poetry readings. Additionally, they could offer specialty pastries and sandwiches that are made in-house with locally sourced ingredients. By offering a unique and personalized experience, this coffee shop could stand out from the competition and attract a loyal customer base.

Wrapping it up, generating successful business ideas requires a combination of creativity, research, and market knowledge. By using a variety of idea generation techniques, evaluation tools, and market research methods, entrepreneurs can identify and select the best ideas, and create successful businesses that meet the needs of their customers and stakeholders.

Chapter 3: Building a Business Plan

"Building a business without a plan is like going on a journey without a map - you might get lucky and stumble upon your destination, but you're more likely to get lost along the way."

A business plan is a written document that outlines an entrepreneur's vision for their business. It serves as a roadmap for the entrepreneur and provides a detailed plan for achieving their goals. A well-crafted business plan is an essential tool for securing funding, recruiting team members, and guiding the growth of the business.

Defining the Business Model

The first step in creating a business plan is to define the business model. This involves identifying the target market, the product or service being offered, and the unique value proposition that sets the business apart from competitors. The business model should also include information on how the product or service will be sold, distributed, and delivered to customers.

Here are a few examples of business models.

1. Subscription model: This model charges customers a recurring fee to access a product or service on a regular basis, such as a magazine subscription or a software-as-a-service (SaaS) product.

2. Freemium model: This model offers a basic version of a product or service for free, but charges for premium features or upgrades. For example, a mobile game might be free to download and play but offer in-app purchases for additional content.

3. Pay-per-use model: This model charges customers based on how much they use a product or service, such as a ride-sharing service that charges by the mile or minute.

4. Marketplace model: This model connects buyers and sellers on a platform and takes a commission or fee for each transaction. Examples include eBay, Etsy, and Airbnb.

5. Direct sales model: This model involves selling products or services directly to customers through a sales team or independent distributors. Examples include Avon and Tupperware.

6. Franchise model: This model involves selling the right to use a company's branding, products, and business model to individual franchisees who operate their own locations. Examples include McDonald's and Subway.

Creating a Marketing Strategy

Once the business model has been defined, entrepreneurs should develop a marketing strategy. This includes identifying the target market, developing a pricing strategy, and creating a promotional plan. The marketing strategy should also outline the channels through which the product or service will be promoted and the tactics that will be used to drive customer engagement and sales.

Some of the key steps in creating a marketing strategy include:

1. Identifying the target market: This involves defining the ideal customer or audience for the product or service and understanding their preferences and behaviors.

2. Developing a unique value proposition: This involves identifying what sets the product or service apart from competitors and how it solves a particular problem or meets a specific need.

Chapter 2: Conducting Market Research

"Market research is the compass that guides entrepreneurs towards their customers' needs and desires."

Market research is an essential component of the entrepreneurial process. It allows entrepreneurs to understand the needs and preferences of their target customers, as well as the dynamics of the market and the competition. In this chapter, we will explore various methods for conducting market research and how to use the insights gained to inform business decisions.

Understanding Customer Needs and Preferences

To create a successful business, entrepreneurs must have a deep understanding of their target customers. This involves understanding their needs, preferences, and behaviors. One way to gain this understanding is through customer interviews and surveys.

Customer interviews can provide valuable insights into the pain points and challenges customers are experiencing. By listening to customers and gathering their feedback, entrepreneurs can identify opportunities to create products and services that meet their needs.

Say, a startup wants to create a new meal delivery service for busy professionals. To better understand the needs and pain points of their potential customers, they conduct a series of customer interviews.

During these interviews, they learn that many busy professionals struggle to find healthy meal options that are both convenient and affordable. They also learn that many people are looking for more variety in their meals and are interested in trying new and exotic cuisines.

Based on this feedback, the startup decides to differentiate themselves by offering a wider variety of healthy meal options, including international cuisine, at an affordable price point. They also make sure to emphasize the convenience of their service, with options for delivery or pickup at multiple locations throughout the city.

By conducting customer interviews and listening carefully to their feedback, the startup can develop a service that meets the needs of their target market and differentiates them from their competition.

Surveys are another effective way to gather information about customer needs and preferences. Surveys can be used to gather quantitative data, such as demographic information and purchasing behavior, as well as qualitative data, such as feedback on product features and customer service.

Here is a brief explanation of the steps involved in creating your own survey:

1. Define the research objectives: Before creating a survey, it's important to define what you want to learn from it. What specific questions do you want to answer?

2. Design the survey: Decide on the format of the survey, such as multiple-choice questions, open-ended questions, or a combination of both. Make sure the questions are clear and easy to understand and avoid leading or biased questions.

3. Choose a survey tool: There are a variety of online survey tools available, such as SurveyMonkey, Google Forms, and Typeform. Choose a tool that fits your needs and budget.

4. Deploy the survey: Determine the best way to distribute the survey to your target audience, such as via email, social media, or in-person. Make sure to provide clear instructions and a deadline for completing the survey.

5. Analyze the results: Once you've collected responses, use the survey tool's analysis features to analyze the data and draw conclusions. Look for patterns and trends in the data that can help you make informed decisions about your business.

Analyzing Competitors and Market Trends

Understanding the competition and the dynamics of the market is also critical for success. This involves analyzing the strengths and weaknesses of competitors, as well as market trends and dynamics.

Competitive analysis involves gathering information about the key players in the market, their products and services, and their strengths and weaknesses. This information can be used to identify opportunities for differentiation and to develop a unique value proposition.

Here's an example of competitive analysis for a hypothetical food delivery app:

Competitor: Grubhub

Strengths:

- Established brand recognition
- Large network of restaurant partners
- User-friendly mobile app

Weaknesses:

- Reports of high commission fees for restaurant partners
- Inconsistent delivery times and order accuracy
- Limited delivery area in some regions

Opportunities:

- Partnering with additional restaurants and expanding delivery area
- Offering more personalized and targeted marketing to customers
- Providing a more seamless user experience

Threats:

- Growing competition from other food delivery apps
- Increasing regulatory scrutiny and potential legal challenges
- Changing consumer preferences or economic conditions

To conduct a competitive analysis, you can research their competitors through a variety of methods, such as visiting their websites, reviewing their marketing materials, analyzing their product offerings, and monitoring their social media presence. You can also gather information from industry reports and trade publications, as well as by attending industry events and conferences. Additionally, you can consider hiring a market research firm to conduct a more in-depth analysis.

Market analysis involves gathering data about the size and characteristics of the market, as well as trends and dynamics. This information can be used to identify opportunities for growth, as well as potential threats or challenges.

Conducting Surveys, Focus Groups, and Other Research Methods

There are a variety of methods that can be used to conduct market research, including surveys, focus groups, and online research.

As mentioned earlier surveys can be conducted online or in person and can provide both quantitative and qualitative data. Focus groups involve bringing together a small group of customers to discuss their experiences and preferences. This method can provide rich, qualitative data, but is typically more expensive and time-consuming.

Online research involves gathering data from online sources, such as social media, forums, and review sites. This method can provide valuable insights into customer feedback and preferences, as well as trends in the market.

Just remember, conducting market research is a critical component of the entrepreneurial process. By understanding customer needs and preferences, analyzing competitors and market trends, and using a variety of research methods, entrepreneurs can gather valuable insights that can inform business decisions and lead to success in the market.

Using Market Research to Make Business Decisions

Once market research has been conducted, the insights gained can be used to make informed business decisions. Entrepreneurs can use the data to refine their product offerings, develop pricing strategies, and create targeted marketing campaigns.

For example, if market research indicates that customers are dissatisfied with a particular feature of a product, the entrepreneur can use that information to make changes to the product or service. Similarly, if market research indicates that customers are willing to pay a premium for a certain feature, the entrepreneur can use that information to develop a pricing strategy that maximizes profitability.

Market research can also be used to inform marketing and advertising campaigns. By understanding customer preferences and behaviors, entrepreneurs can create targeted campaigns that resonate with their target audience.

In addition to using market research to inform business decisions, entrepreneurs can also use it to measure the success of their efforts. By gathering data on key metrics such as customer satisfaction and market share, entrepreneurs can evaluate the effectiveness of their strategies and adjust as needed.

Challenges and Limitations of Market Research

While market research can provide valuable insights, it is important to recognize that there are limitations and challenges associated with the process. One of the biggest challenges is gathering accurate and representative data. If the sample size is too small or unrepresentative of the target market, the insights gained may not be accurate or useful.

Another challenge is the potential for bias in the research process. This can occur if the research questions are biased or if the sample is not random. To mitigate this risk, it is important to use a variety of research methods and to ensure that the research questions are unbiased and objective.

Finally, market research can be time-consuming and expensive. Conducting surveys, focus groups, and other research methods can be resource-intensive, and it may take time to gather and analyze the data.

In short, market research is a critical component of the entrepreneurial process. By using a variety of research methods, entrepreneurs can gain valuable insights into customer needs and preferences, as well as market trends and competition. These insights can be used to inform business decisions and measure the success of strategies over time. While market research can be challenging and expensive, it is a necessary investment for any entrepreneur looking to create a successful business.

Entrepreneurs should also assess the financial feasibility of their ideas during the idea generation phase. This includes evaluating the costs associated with developing and launching the product or service, as well as potential revenue streams and profitability.

To assess costs, entrepreneurs can create a detailed budget that considers all expenses associated with product development, manufacturing, marketing, and sales. This will help to identify potential cost savings opportunities and to ensure that the product can be produced and sold at a profit.

Assessing revenue streams and profitability involves identifying potential customers and estimating the price they are willing to pay for the product or service. Entrepreneurs should also consider factors such as market size and competition, as these can impact the potential for revenue and profitability.

Additionally, it is important to have a clear understanding of the costs involved in producing and delivering the product or service, including direct costs such as materials and labor, as well as indirect costs such as rent and utilities. By analyzing these factors, entrepreneurs can make informed decisions about pricing and target markets and develop a realistic financial plan that considers the potential risks and challenges of launching and growing a successful business.

3. Determining the marketing mix: This involves selecting the appropriate channels and tactics for promoting the product or service, such as advertising, content marketing, social media, and public relations.

4. Setting a budget: This involves determining how much to spend on marketing efforts and how to allocate resources effectively.

5. Measuring and evaluating results: This involves tracking the success of the marketing strategy and adjusting it as needed to maximize its effectiveness.

Developing Financial Projections and Budgets

Another critical component of the business plan is the financial projections and budgets. This involves forecasting the revenue and expenses of the business over a set period, typically three to five years. Entrepreneurs should also create a detailed budget that includes all expenses associated with launching and operating the business.

Financial projections and budgets should be based on realistic assumptions about market demand, competition, and operational costs. It is important to be conservative in these projections and to build in a buffer for unexpected expenses or changes in market conditions.

Here are the steps to developing financial projections and budgets for a business plan:

1. Estimate revenue: Start by estimating the total amount of revenue you expect to generate. This can be based on market research, industry benchmarks, or your own experience.

2. Determine expenses: Create a list of all your expenses, including fixed costs (such as rent and salaries) and variable costs (such as marketing and supplies). Use historical data or market research to estimate these costs.

3. Calculate profit: Once you have estimated your revenue and expenses, subtract the total expenses from the total revenue to calculate your profit. This will help you determine whether your business is viable.

4. Develop cash flow projections: In addition to profit and loss projections, you should also develop cash flow projections. This will help you determine

whether you will have enough cash on hand to pay bills and other expenses.

5. Set financial goals: Based on your financial projections, set realistic financial goals for your business. This can include revenue targets, profitability targets, or other metrics that are important to your business.

6. Monitor and adjust: Once you have developed your financial projections and budgets, it's important to monitor your actual results and adjust your projections as needed. This will help you stay on track and make informed decisions about your business.

Next, we will discuss additional components of a business plan, including operations, team structure, and risk management. By the end of this chapter, entrepreneurs should have a clear understanding of what goes into a well-crafted business plan and how to use it to guide the growth of their business.

Operations, Team Structure, and Risk Management

The operations section of the business plan outlines how the business will be run on a day-to-day basis. This includes information on the location of the business, the equipment and technology needed to produce the product or service, and the processes and systems that will be used to manage operations.

The team structure section of the business plan outlines the roles and responsibilities of the leadership team and any employees or contractors that will be hired. This section should also include information on the hiring process, the compensation and benefits package, and any training or development programs that will be offered to team members.

An example of the team structure section of a business plan might look like this:

Leadership Team:

- CEO: Responsible for overall business strategy, fundraising, and executive decision making

- CMO: Responsible for developing and implementing marketing strategy, managing the brand, and analyzing market trends

- CFO: Responsible for financial strategy, budgeting, and forecasting

Employee Roles:

- Sales team: Responsible for generating revenue by selling the company's products or services

- Operations team: Responsible for managing day-to-day business operations, such as logistics, production, and customer service

- Product development team: Responsible for creating and refining the company's products or services

- IT team: Responsible for managing the company's technology infrastructure and ensuring data security

This section of the business plan helps potential investors or partners understand the business's organizational structure and the team's roles and responsibilities. It can also be used as a roadmap for building the team and expanding the business as it grows.

The risk management section of the business plan identifies potential risks and challenges that the business may face and outlines strategies for mitigating those risks. This may include information on legal and regulatory compliance, intellectual property protection, and contingency plans for unforeseen events such as natural disasters or economic downturns.

An example of the risk management section of a business plan might include:

Risk: Economic downturn Impact: Decrease in customer spending and revenue Mitigation Strategy: Develop contingency plans for cost-cutting measures, such as reducing staff hours or shifting to lower-cost suppliers, in the event of an economic downturn. Diversify revenue streams by offering complementary products or services that are less affected by economic conditions.

Risk: Cybersecurity breach Impact: Compromised sensitive data, loss of customer trust and loyalty Mitigation Strategy: Invest in robust cybersecurity measures, including firewalls, encryption, and regular system backups. Train employees on best practices for data security and implement policies for regular system updates and maintenance.

Risk: Supply chain disruption Impact: Delayed or interrupted production, inability to meet customer demand Mitigation Strategy: Develop relationships with multiple suppliers to reduce dependence on any single source. Monitor supplier performance and identify potential issues early. Maintain safety stock levels of critical supplies and implement a contingency plan for alternative suppliers in case of disruption.

By identifying potential risks and outlining strategies to mitigate those risks, the business can be better prepared to navigate challenges and continue operating successfully.

Putting it All Together

A well-crafted business plan is essential for guiding the growth of a new venture. It should be detailed and comprehensive, yet easy to read and understand. Entrepreneurs should take the time to research and analyze each component of the plan, and to revise it as needed based on feedback from mentors, investors, and other stakeholders.

In the next chapter, we will discuss how to fund a new venture, including bootstrapping, crowdfunding, and venture capital. By the end of this section, entrepreneurs should have a clear understanding of the various funding options available to them and how to choose the best option for their business.

Chapter 4: Funding the Business

"Investment is not just a transaction, but a partnership in the journey of bringing a vision to life."

Starting a new venture requires capital, and entrepreneurs need to identify and secure funding to turn their ideas into reality. In this chapter, we will explore the various sources of funding available to entrepreneurs, including loans, grants, and investments. We will also discuss how to pitch to investors and secure funding, as well as how to manage finances and cash flow to ensure the long-term success of the business.

Sources of Funding

There are various sources of funding available to entrepreneurs, and it is important to understand the advantages and disadvantages of each option. Loans are a common source of funding, and they can be obtained from banks, government agencies, and other financial institutions. Loans typically require collateral and come with interest rates and repayment schedules that must be adhered to.

Grants are another source of funding and are typically offered by government agencies and non-profit organizations. Grants do not need to be repaid but often come with specific requirements and restrictions on how the funds can be used.

Investments are a third source of funding and can come from individual investors, venture capital firms, or angel investors. In exchange for their investment, investors typically receive equity in the company and may also provide guidance and support to the entrepreneur.

Here are a few examples of how to find sources of funding for a business:

1. Bank loans: A traditional source of funding is a bank loan, which can be secured or unsecured. This requires a good credit score and a solid business plan.

2. Angel investors: Angel investors are individuals who invest in startups in exchange for equity in the company. These investors often have experience in the industry and can provide valuable guidance and advice.

3. Venture capital: Venture capital firms invest in startups with high-growth potential. In exchange for funding, they typically require a percentage of ownership in the company.

4. Crowdfunding: Crowdfunding platforms like Kickstarter or Indiegogo allow businesses to raise funds from a large number of people. This can be a good option for businesses with a strong online presence and a compelling story.

5. Small Business Administration (SBA) loans: The SBA provides loans to small businesses through approved lenders. These loans often have lower interest rates and longer repayment terms than traditional bank loans.

Pitching to Investors and Securing Funding

To secure funding, entrepreneurs need to be able to pitch their ideas effectively to investors. This involves creating a compelling pitch deck that outlines the business model, market opportunity, and financial projections. The pitch deck should be clear, concise, and visually engaging, and should also address potential risks and challenges.

Once the pitch deck is prepared, entrepreneurs can begin reaching out to potential investors. This may involve attending networking events, reaching out to contacts in the industry, or working with a broker or investment bank. When meeting with investors, entrepreneurs should be prepared to answer questions about the business and to provide additional information as needed.

here's an example of how a startup might pitch to investors and secure funding:

John, the founder of a tech startup, is seeking funding to grow his company. He has identified a group of potential investors who are interested in his industry and has set up a meeting with them to pitch his business idea. During the pitch, John presents the following information:

- A brief overview of the company, including the mission and vision.
- A description of the problem his company is solving, and the market opportunity that exists.
- An explanation of the product or service his company offers, and how it is different from existing solutions in the market.
- An outline of the company's financials, including revenue projections and current burn rate.
- A discussion of the team, highlighting their skills and experience.
- An explanation of how the investment will be used to grow the business and increase revenue.

John answers questions from the investors and provides additional information as needed. He also shares his pitch deck and other relevant materials to help the investors better understand his business.

If the investors are interested in the opportunity, John will negotiate the terms of the investment and work to secure the funding needed to take his business to the next level.

You may not always have your pitch deck with you. An elevator pitch is a brief and concise introduction to your business that you can deliver in the time it takes to ride an elevator. It is a powerful tool for making a great first impression and generating interest in your business.

To create an effective elevator pitch, start with a strong opening that captures the listener's attention and clearly communicates the problem your business solves. For example, "Our company is focused on developing sustainable and environmentally friendly products for the home and workplace."

Next, explain your solution and how it is unique or innovative. This could include features, benefits, or advantages over other products in the market. For example,

"Our products are made with 100% recycled materials, making them not only eco-friendly but also durable and cost-effective."

Be sure to include a call to action at the end of your pitch, such as asking for a meeting or providing contact information. For example, "I would love the opportunity to share more with you about our products and discuss how we can work together. Here's my card, feel free to contact me any time."

Remember to practice your pitch and tailor it to your audience. Keep it short and sweet, and make sure it is clear and compelling. A well-crafted elevator pitch can help you generate interest and secure funding for your business.

Managing Finances and Cash Flow

Once funding has been secured, it is essential to manage finances and cash flow effectively to ensure the long-term success of the business. This involves creating a budget, monitoring expenses and revenue, and staying on top of accounts payable and accounts receivable.

Entrepreneurs should also develop a plan for managing cash flow, including strategies for dealing with seasonal fluctuations, unexpected expenses, and other challenges that may arise. This may involve setting aside reserves or establishing a line of credit with a financial institution.

Here's an example of developing a plan for managing cash flow in a business plan:

Cash Flow Management Plan:

The cash flow management plan for our business will focus on maintaining a positive cash flow throughout the year, while also preparing for any unexpected expenses or seasonal fluctuations that may occur. The following strategies will be implemented to achieve this goal:

1. Maintain a cash reserve: We will establish a cash reserve to cover unexpected expenses, as well as any fluctuations in revenue that may occur during the year. This cash reserve will be maintained in a separate account and will only be used for emergencies.

2. Monitor cash flow: We will closely monitor our cash flow on a monthly basis to ensure that we are meeting our financial goals. We will use

accounting software to track our cash flow and generate financial reports to keep us informed.

3. Control expenses: We will carefully manage our expenses to ensure that we are not overspending and depleting our cash reserves. This will include reviewing all expenses regularly and cutting back on any unnecessary expenditures.

4. Manage accounts receivable: We will implement a system for managing accounts receivable, including setting up payment terms with customers and following up on any late payments.

5. Forecast future cash flow: We will develop a detailed cash flow forecast that takes into account expected revenue and expenses for the next year. This will help us to identify potential shortfalls and take action to prevent them.

By implementing these strategies, we are confident that we can manage our cash flow effectively and maintain a positive financial position throughout the year.

In the second half of this chapter, we will discuss additional strategies for managing finances and cash flow, including financial reporting and forecasting. By the end of this section, entrepreneurs should have a clear understanding of how to secure funding and manage finances effectively to ensure the long-term success of their business.

Financial Reporting and Forecasting

In addition to managing finances and cash flow, entrepreneurs should also develop a system for financial reporting and forecasting. Financial reporting involves tracking and analyzing financial data, such as revenue, expenses, and profit margins. This information can be used to make informed decisions about the future of the business, such as whether to invest in new products or services, expand into new markets, or make changes to the existing operations.

Financial forecasting involves using historical financial data to predict future revenue and expenses. This can be useful for setting long-term goals and creating budgets, as well as for identifying potential risks and challenges. Entrepreneurs should regularly review and update their financial forecasts to ensure that they are on track to meet their goals.

Developing a system for financial reporting and forecasting involves the following steps:

1. Choose a financial reporting software or system that meets the needs of the business. This could be a cloud-based accounting software, a spreadsheet program, or a dedicated financial reporting system.

2. Set up the system to accurately capture all financial transactions, including revenue, expenses, and assets.

3. Create regular financial reports that provide an overview of the business's financial health, including cash flow, profitability, and expenses.

4. Use these reports to identify areas where the business can improve its financial performance, such as by reducing expenses or increasing revenue.

5. Develop a forecasting model that predicts future revenue and expenses based on historical data and market trends.

6. Use the forecasting model to plan for future investments, expansions, and other initiatives, and to identify potential risks and challenges that may arise.

7. Continuously monitor and adjust the financial reporting and forecasting system as necessary to ensure that it remains accurate, relevant, and effective in helping the business achieve its financial goals.

There are many tools available to help with financial reporting and forecasting. Some popular options include accounting software such as QuickBooks or Xero, financial modeling software such as Excel or Google Sheets, and business intelligence tools such as Tableau or Power BI. Additionally, some companies may choose to work with financial advisors or consultants to help them with their financial reporting and forecasting needs.

In sum, funding a new venture is a critical part of the entrepreneurial process, and it requires careful planning, preparation, and execution. By understanding the various sources of funding available, creating a compelling pitch deck, and managing finances and cash flow effectively, entrepreneurs can increase their chances of success and position their business for long-term growth.

In the next chapter, we will discuss how to build a strong team and develop effective leadership skills. This includes information on hiring and training employees, managing team dynamics, and creating a culture of innovation and collaboration. By the end of this section, entrepreneurs should have a clear understanding of how to build a team that can help them achieve their goals and drive the success of their business.

Chapter 5: Launching the Business

"Launch with intention, not just ambition, and you'll be on the path to a successful mission."

Entrepreneurs invest a significant amount of time and resources into bringing their ideas to life, and launching the business is a critical step in the entrepreneurial process. This chapter will cover the key steps involved in launching a business, including preparing for launch day, establishing a brand, and generating revenue.

Preparing for Launch Day

Launching a business requires careful planning and execution. Entrepreneurs should create a detailed launch plan that outlines the steps involved in bringing the product or service to market. This may include setting a launch date, identifying distribution channels, preparing marketing materials, and training staff. The launch plan should be reviewed and revised as necessary to ensure that all aspects of the launch are well-coordinated and executed.

An example of a launch plan for a new product:

1. Set a launch date: Determine the date on which the product will be released to the market.

2. Identify target customers: Define the demographic that the product will serve and identify the specific needs and desires of that group.

3. Develop a marketing strategy: Create a comprehensive marketing plan that will reach the target customers through various channels, such as social media, email marketing, and paid advertising.

4. Create product packaging and branding: Develop an eye-catching and memorable design for the product's packaging and branding that will differentiate it from competitors.

5. Establish a pricing strategy: Determine the price of the product that will be competitive in the market and provide the desired profit margin.

6. Prepare the product for distribution: Ensure that the product is manufactured and packaged according to specifications and that it is ready for distribution by the launch date.

7. Organize a launch event: Plan and host a launch event to generate excitement and media coverage for the product.

8. Monitor and measure success: Track the success of the product launch through metrics such as sales, customer feedback, and media coverage. Use this information to adjust the marketing strategy and improve the product.

For example, a new coffee shop owner may create a detailed launch plan that includes tasks such as hiring staff, ordering equipment and supplies, designing the store layout, and promoting the grand opening. The owner might also set deadlines for each task and allocate resources, such as time and money, to ensure that the plan is executed smoothly. By following this plan, the coffee shop owner can increase the chances of a successful launch and build a strong foundation for the business.

Establishing a Brand and Marketing the Business

A strong brand is critical to the success of any business, as it helps to differentiate the product or service from competitors and communicates the value proposition to customers. Entrepreneurs should develop a brand strategy that defines the business's unique value proposition, target audience, and messaging. This may involve creating a brand identity, including a logo, tagline, and brand guidelines, as well as developing marketing materials such as a website, social media profiles, and advertising campaigns.

For example, When Sarah started her bakery business, she knew that establishing a strong brand would be key to standing out in a crowded market. She spent months carefully considering the look and feel of her brand, from the colors and fonts to the messaging and tone of voice.

To create buzz around her launch, Sarah held a pop-up event where she gave away free samples of her signature baked goods. She also leveraged social media to build a following, sharing behind-the-scenes photos of her baking process and engaging with her audience in the comments.

Through these efforts, Sarah was able to build a loyal customer base and generate word-of-mouth buzz around her brand. Her carefully crafted brand and marketing strategy helped her business stand out in a competitive market and establish a reputation for quality and excellence.

Building a Customer Base and Generating Revenue

Once the business is launched, the focus shifts to building a customer base and generating revenue. Entrepreneurs should develop a sales and marketing strategy that is aligned with their target audience and business goals. This may involve identifying potential customers, creating marketing campaigns, and developing a sales process that converts leads into customers. Additionally, entrepreneurs should continually monitor and evaluate their sales and marketing efforts to identify areas for improvement and refine their approach over time.

Consider this example. Jen started a small business selling handmade soap online. She had a great product and a lot of passion, but after a few months, she realized that she was struggling to generate sales. Jen decided to focus on building her customer base and generating revenue, and she came up with a plan.

First, Jen reached out to bloggers and influencers in the beauty and wellness space to ask if they would review her products. She sent them free samples and asked them to share their honest opinions on their blogs and social media channels. This helped her get her products in front of a wider audience and generate some buzz.

Next, Jen started attending local craft fairs and farmers markets. She set up a booth with samples of her soaps and talked to customers about her products. This gave her the chance to get direct feedback from customers and build relationships with them.

Finally, Jen started offering discounts and promotions to her email list and social media followers. She ran a holiday sale and offered free shipping on orders over a certain amount. This helped her generate more sales and get more people interested in her brand.

Thanks to these efforts, Jen was able to build a loyal customer base and generate consistent revenue. Her business grew steadily over time, and she was able to quit her day job and focus on her business full-time.

In the next section, we will discuss the importance of maintaining a focus on innovation and continuous improvement. This includes information on developing a culture of experimentation, seeking customer feedback, and incorporating new technologies and trends into the business. By the end of this chapter, entrepreneurs should have a clear understanding of how to successfully launch their business and begin generating revenue.

Fostering Innovation and Continuous Improvement

The launch of a new business is just the beginning, and successful entrepreneurs understand the importance of maintaining a focus on innovation and continuous improvement. This involves creating a culture of experimentation and learning, seeking customer feedback, and incorporating new technologies and trends into the business.

Here's an example. John runs a small software development company that specializes in creating mobile apps for small businesses. When he first started the company, he had a vision for creating an app that would revolutionize the way small businesses managed their inventory. However, after launching the app and receiving feedback from his customers, he realized that there were many other areas in which small businesses needed help.

Rather than sticking to his original vision, John decided to pivot and expand the focus of the company to include a suite of business management tools for small businesses. He regularly met with his team to brainstorm new ideas and features, and he also sought input from his customers to identify pain points and areas for improvement.

As a result of his commitment to innovation and continuous improvement, John's company has become a leader in the industry, with a loyal customer base and a reputation for delivering high-quality products that meet the needs of small businesses.

Creating a Culture of Experimentation

Innovation requires a willingness to take risks and experiment with new ideas. Entrepreneurs should create a culture that encourages experimentation and learning and provides support for new ideas and initiatives. This may involve setting aside time for team members to work on new projects, providing resources for research and development, and celebrating successes and failures as learning opportunities.

One example is Google. From its early days, Google has encouraged its employees to take risks and experiment with new ideas. For example, Google famously allows its engineers to spend 20% of their time on personal projects, which has resulted in some of the company's most successful products, including Gmail and Google News.

Google also fosters a culture of continuous improvement by using data to drive decision-making. The company collects and analyzes vast amounts of data on user behavior, which it uses to refine its products and services. Google also uses a variety of testing and optimization techniques, such as A/B testing, to experiment with different ideas and approaches.

Through its emphasis on experimentation and data-driven decision-making, Google has been able to stay at the forefront of innovation and maintain its competitive edge in the fast-paced tech industry.

Seeking Customer Feedback

Customer feedback is a valuable source of information for entrepreneurs, as it provides insight into the customer experience and identifies areas for improvement. Entrepreneurs should actively seek out customer feedback through surveys, focus groups, and other channels, and use this information to make informed decisions about the direction of the business.

One example of a company seeking customer feedback is Airbnb. As a platform that relies heavily on customer satisfaction, Airbnb has made it a priority to collect feedback from both guests and hosts to continually improve their services.

To gather feedback, Airbnb uses various methods such as surveys and reviews. After each stay, guests are asked to leave a review and rating of their experience, which is then shared with the host and made public on the platform. Hosts are also given the opportunity to rate their guests and provide feedback.

In addition to these methods, Airbnb also conducts regular surveys to gather more detailed feedback from both guests and hosts. This feedback is used to identify areas for improvement and to inform product development.

By actively seeking customer feedback, Airbnb has been able to improve its platform and create a better experience for both guests and hosts, which has contributed to its success as a business.

Incorporating New Technologies and Trends

Technological advancements and changing market trends can create new opportunities for entrepreneurs to innovate and improve their business. Entrepreneurs should stay up to date on new technologies and trends in their industry and be willing to adopt new approaches and tools as they emerge. This may involve incorporating new software or hardware into the business, developing new products or services, or rethinking the business model to better align with changing customer needs.

Incorporating new technologies and trends can be a critical step for businesses to remain competitive and meet the evolving needs of their customers. One example of a company successfully incorporating new technologies is Amazon. In 2016, Amazon launched Amazon Go, a checkout-free store where customers could simply walk in, pick up the items they wanted, and walk out. The store uses a range of technologies, including computer vision, deep learning algorithms, and sensor fusion to track customers' movements and purchases, enabling them to shop without the need to interact with a cashier or self-checkout machine.

Amazon Go has been successful in meeting customers' needs for a faster and more convenient shopping experience, and the company has continued to innovate and incorporate new technologies to enhance the customer experience, such as its Just Walk Out technology that is now being offered to other retailers. By staying on top of emerging technologies and trends and incorporating them into their operations, companies like Amazon can maintain a competitive edge and continue to grow and succeed.

To wrap it up, launching a new business is a complex and challenging process, but it can also be incredibly rewarding for entrepreneurs who are willing to put in the time and effort required for success. By preparing carefully, establishing a strong brand, building a customer base, and fostering a culture of innovation and continuous improvement, entrepreneurs can position their business for long-term growth and success. In the next chapter, we will discuss how to manage growth and scale the business, including information on hiring and training new staff, developing new products and services, and expanding into new markets.

Chapter 6: Growing the Business

"A successful business is not built in a day, but through persistent efforts and a relentless drive to innovate and improve."

As a business gains momentum and becomes established in the market, entrepreneurs must focus on strategies for growth and expansion. This involves scaling operations, building a strong team, and developing partnerships and collaborations with other businesses.

Scaling the Business and Expanding Operations

In its early stages, Airbnb was just a platform for people to list and rent out their homes or apartments to travelers. However, over time, the company has expanded its offerings to include experiences, adventures, and other unique travel opportunities.

To scale and expand its business, Airbnb has invested heavily in its technology infrastructure and user experience, making it easier for hosts and guests to find and book accommodations and experiences. The company has also worked to establish partnerships with local governments and tourism boards, which has helped to increase its credibility and visibility in new markets.

In addition to its core business, Airbnb has also launched new initiatives, such as Airbnb for Work, which caters to business travelers, and Airbnb Plus, a collection of high-end accommodations. These efforts have helped the company to diversify its revenue streams and tap into new markets.

By constantly innovating and expanding its offerings, Airbnb has been able to stay ahead of the competition and maintain its position as a leader in the travel industry.

Scaling a business involves expanding operations and increasing revenue while maintaining the quality and efficiency that allowed the business to succeed in the first place. This may involve increasing production, expanding the customer base, opening new locations, or entering new markets. Entrepreneurs must carefully consider the risks and benefits of each growth strategy and ensure that they have the resources and infrastructure in place to support expansion.

Hiring Employees and Building a Team

As a business grows, entrepreneurs must hire new staff and build a team that can support increased production and operations. This requires careful consideration of the skills and experience needed to support the business, as well as a focus on culture and values to ensure that new hires align with the company's mission and vision.

When it comes to hiring employees and building a team, there are several best practices that can help ensure that the right people are brought on board and that they are able to work together effectively. Here is an example of how a company might approach this process:

A growing technology startup has been operating with a small team of founders for the past year, but they are now ready to bring on additional employees to help take the company to the next level. They start by identifying the key roles that need to be filled, which include a software engineer, a marketing specialist, and an operations manager.

Next, the company creates job postings and begins advertising them through a variety of channels, including social media, job boards, and industry-specific publications. They also reach out to their network of contacts to ask for referrals and recommendations.

As applications start to come in, the company reviews each one carefully to determine which candidates have the most relevant skills and experience. They also look for candidates who are a good cultural fit and who are passionate about the company's mission.

For each open position, the company schedules a series of interviews with top candidates, which may include phone interviews, in-person interviews, and skills assessments. During these interviews, they ask a range of questions to assess the candidate's technical skills, communication skills, problem-solving abilities, and team fit.

Once the interviews are complete, the company selects the top candidate for each position and extends an offer. They work with the new hires to ensure that they have a smooth onboarding process and that they have access to the resources they need to be successful in their roles.

Over time, the company continues to invest in its employees by providing ongoing training and development opportunities, fostering a culture of collaboration and innovation, and offering competitive compensation and benefits packages. This helps to ensure that the team remains motivated and engaged, and that the company is well-positioned for long-term success.

Developing Partnerships and Collaborations

One example of a company developing partnerships and collaborations is the collaboration between Apple and Nike to create the Nike+ iPod Sport Kit. The two companies came together to combine their respective expertise in technology and athletic apparel to create a product that allowed runners to track their progress through their iPods. The product was a success, and the collaboration between the two companies helped to boost sales for both. This partnership allowed Nike to tap into Apple's loyal customer base, while Apple was able to expand into the athletic market.

Collaborating with other businesses can provide new opportunities for growth and expansion, as well as access to new resources and expertise. Entrepreneurs may consider partnerships with suppliers, distributors, or other businesses in their industry, as well as collaborations with non-profits, government agencies, or academic institutions to support research and development.

In the second half of this chapter, we will discuss strategies for managing growth, including developing new products and services, implementing new technologies, and building a strong brand that can support expansion into new markets.

Managing Growth

As a business expands and evolves, entrepreneurs must continue to innovate and adapt to changing market conditions. This involves developing new products and services, implementing new technologies, and building a strong brand that can support expansion into new markets.

One example of how a company can manage growth is by creating a strategic plan that outlines the steps and milestones for achieving growth targets. This plan should consider the company's strengths and weaknesses, the competitive landscape, market trends, and customer needs. It should also identify the resources required to achieve growth, such as capital, talent, technology, and infrastructure.

For instance, let's consider the example of a software development company that has experienced significant growth in recent years. In order to manage this growth effectively, the company developed a strategic plan that included the following steps:

1. Assess the market: The company conducted a thorough analysis of the market, including the competitive landscape, customer needs, and market trends. This helped them identify potential growth opportunities and areas where they could differentiate themselves from competitors.

2. Invest in technology and infrastructure: The company invested in new technology and infrastructure to support their growth, including upgrading their server capacity and expanding their software development team.

3. Hire new talent: The company hired new talent to support their growing client base, including developers, project managers, and sales and marketing professionals.

4. Expand into new markets: The company expanded into new markets by partnering with local businesses and attending industry events to increase their visibility.

5. Implement a performance management system: The company implemented a performance management system to ensure that their

employees were aligned with the company's growth objectives and had the necessary skills and resources to achieve them.

By following this strategic plan, the company was able to manage its growth effectively and continue to meet the needs of its clients while remaining competitive in the market.

Developing New Products and Services

XYZ Corp is a technology company that has been successful in developing a suite of software products that are used by small businesses. As the company grows, the leadership team is constantly looking for opportunities to expand their product offerings and reach new markets.

To do this, they regularly hold brainstorming sessions with their development team to generate new ideas for products and features that can be added to their existing suite. They also keep a close eye on emerging technologies and trends, such as AI and machine learning, to see how they can be incorporated into their products.

One new product that they developed was a mobile app that allows small business owners to manage their inventory on the go. The app integrates with their existing software products and provides real-time updates on inventory levels, sales data, and other key metrics. This product was well-received by their existing customer base and helped them attract new customers who were looking for mobile solutions.

In addition to developing new products, XYZ Corp also places a strong emphasis on continuous improvement of their existing products. They regularly gather feedback from their customers to identify areas for improvement and implement new features and updates to meet their needs. This has helped them maintain a strong competitive edge and continue to grow their customer base over time.

Successful businesses are constantly innovating and developing new products and services that meet the evolving needs of their customers. Entrepreneurs should be attuned to market trends and customer feedback to identify opportunities for new product or service offerings. They must also carefully consider the resources and infrastructure needed to support new product development, as well as the potential risks and rewards associated with innovation.

Implementing New Technologies

Technological advancements are transforming industries and creating new opportunities for growth and innovation. Entrepreneurs must stay up to date with emerging technologies and consider how they can be leveraged to improve operations, increase efficiency, and enhance the customer experience. This may involve investing in new software, hardware, or other technology solutions, as well as hiring staff with the technical expertise needed to support these new systems.

One example of the importance of staying up to date with emerging technologies is the rise of e-commerce and the impact it has had on traditional brick-and-mortar businesses. As more and more consumers turn to online shopping, businesses that have not adapted to this trend risk losing customers and falling behind the competition.

For instance, a small retail store owner who embraced e-commerce technologies such as online stores, social media marketing, and other digital tools have been able to reach customers from all over the world, and as a result, significantly increased their sales and revenue. In contrast, another retail store that ignored these emerging technologies struggled to compete, lost market share, and eventually went out of business.

Thus, by keeping abreast of emerging technologies, entrepreneurs can identify new opportunities and stay ahead of their competitors, and ultimately thrive in an ever-changing business landscape.

Building a Strong Brand

A strong brand can be a powerful asset for a growing business. Entrepreneurs must carefully consider their branding strategy, including the company's values, messaging, and visual identity, to ensure that it resonates with their target audience and effectively differentiates them from competitors. As the business expands into new markets, entrepreneurs must also consider how to adapt their brand strategy to meet the unique needs and preferences of different customer segments.

One example of a company that has successfully built a strong brand is Nike. Nike's "swoosh" logo is recognized around the world, and the company is known for its high-quality athletic footwear, apparel, and equipment. Nike has built its brand by sponsoring high-profile athletes and teams, including Michael Jordan, Tiger Woods, and the Brazilian national soccer team. The company has also invested heavily in marketing campaigns, such as its "Just Do It" campaign, which has become iconic in the advertising world. Through these efforts, Nike has established itself as a leading brand in the sports industry and continues to maintain its strong brand identity.

In the remainder of this chapter, we will discuss strategies for managing the challenges that come with growth, including hiring and managing staff, maintaining financial stability, and adapting to new market conditions. By implementing these strategies, entrepreneurs can successfully navigate the complexities of scaling a business and achieve long-term success.

Managing the Challenges of Growth

As a business grows, entrepreneurs must also manage several challenges related to staffing, financial stability, and market conditions.

Hiring and Managing Staff

As a business expands, it becomes increasingly important to hire and manage a talented and motivated team. Entrepreneurs must develop effective recruiting strategies to attract the best candidates, as well as processes for onboarding, training, and development to ensure that new hires are able to contribute to the business's success. Ongoing management of staff requires effective communication, leadership, and performance management, as well as attention to issues related to employee morale and retention.

Here are a few examples of best practices for hiring and managing staff:

1. Develop a strong employer brand: A company's reputation as an employer can have a significant impact on its ability to attract and retain top talent. Develop a strong employer brand by providing a positive workplace culture, fair compensation, and opportunities for growth and development.

2. Use data-driven hiring practices: Use data to make informed hiring decisions. Develop clear job descriptions, use assessments and testing to

evaluate skills, and consider using artificial intelligence and other emerging technologies to help identify the best candidates.

3. Provide ongoing training and development: Offer opportunities for ongoing training and development to help employees improve their skills and advance their careers. This can help increase employee engagement and retention.

4. Encourage open communication: Create a culture of open communication where employees feel comfortable sharing their ideas and feedback. Regularly solicit input and feedback from staff to identify areas for improvement and address concerns before they become bigger issues.

5. Recognize and reward performance: Recognize and reward employees who perform well, both individually and as part of a team. This can help increase motivation, engagement, and loyalty.

6. Develop a strong leadership team: Invest in developing a strong leadership team that can provide direction and support to employees. This can help ensure that employees have the resources and guidance they need to be successful.

7. Provide work-life balance: Recognize that employees have lives outside of work and offer flexibility in scheduling and work arrangements where possible. This can help reduce stress and increase job satisfaction.

We've all been there. You're and your staff are overworked and in need of a break. But consider how a bad hire and a good hire can impact your business.

Example of a bad hire: A small business owner hires an individual to fill an important role in the company without thoroughly vetting the candidate's qualifications and experience. The individual is disorganized, lacks the necessary skills for the job, and is unable to meet deadlines. The owner spends a significant amount of time training and coaching the individual but ultimately decides to let them go after several months. The company's productivity is negatively impacted, and the owner is forced to spend additional time and resources to find a replacement.

Example of a good hire: A business owner carefully screens and interviews multiple candidates for an open position before selecting a highly qualified individual with relevant experience and a strong work ethic. The new hire quickly becomes an asset to the company, exceeding expectations and contributing to the growth and success of the business. They also work well with the existing team and help to create a positive work culture. The business owner is able to focus on other areas of the company, knowing that the new hire is capable of handling their responsibilities.

Maintaining Financial Stability

In the early 1990s, Apple was struggling financially, and its market share had declined significantly. However, under the leadership of Steve Jobs, the company underwent a major overhaul, streamlining its product line and refocusing on innovation and design.

Apple also adopted a conservative financial strategy, building up a significant cash reserve to weather economic downturns and fund future growth. This allowed the company to make strategic acquisitions, such as the purchase of NeXT and its subsequent integration of Jobs back into the company, which ultimately led to the development of the iPod, iPhone, and other successful products.

In addition, Apple has maintained strong relationships with its suppliers and partners, working closely with them to ensure quality and consistency across its product lines. The company also invests heavily in research and development, which has helped it stay ahead of its competitors in terms of innovation and technology.

Overall, Apple's focus on financial stability, strategic planning, innovation, and strong relationships with its partners has allowed it to maintain its position as a leading technology company and a dominant player in the market.

As a business grows, it becomes increasingly important to maintain financial stability and manage cash flow effectively. Entrepreneurs must develop financial projections and budgets that account for the increased costs associated with growth, as well as strategies for managing debt and securing additional funding if needed. They must also monitor key financial metrics, such as revenue, profit margins, and cash reserves, to ensure that the business remains financially healthy and sustainable.

Adapting to New Market Conditions

As a business grows, it may encounter new market conditions, such as increased competition or changing consumer preferences, that require a shift in strategy. Entrepreneurs must be willing to adapt to these new conditions by re-evaluating their business model, refining their marketing strategy, and exploring new opportunities for growth and expansion.

An example of this may be the local coffee shop that had to adjust its operations during the COVID-19 pandemic. Before the pandemic, the coffee shop relied on in-person sales and foot traffic from the surrounding businesses and neighborhood. However, with the pandemic forcing many people to work from home and many businesses to close or operate at limited capacity, the coffee shop's revenue began to decline.

To adapt, the coffee shop started offering online ordering and delivery services to reach customers who were staying home. They also began selling coffee beans and other merchandise through their website and social media channels. Additionally, the coffee shop started offering outdoor seating and implemented safety protocols to comply with health guidelines.

By adapting their operations to the new market conditions, the coffee shop was able to maintain its customer base and even attract new customers who were looking for ways to support local businesses during the pandemic. This example illustrates the importance of small businesses being able to adapt quickly to changes in the market and being willing to try new things to stay competitive.

Remember, growing a business can be challenging, but with the right strategies in place, entrepreneurs can successfully navigate the complexities of scaling and achieve long-term success. By focusing on developing a strong team, maintaining financial stability, and adapting to changing market conditions, entrepreneurs can build a thriving business that creates value for customers and delivers long-term returns for stakeholders.

Chapter 7: Managing Risks and Challenges

"Entrepreneurship is a game of calculated risks, but those who manage risks and overcome challenges are the ones who emerge victorious."

Starting and running a business is never easy, and entrepreneurs face a range of risks and challenges along the way. From financial challenges to unexpected market shifts, entrepreneurs must be prepared to navigate a variety of obstacles if they want to succeed in the long term.

Identifying and Mitigating Risks

One of the most important tasks for entrepreneurs is to identify and mitigate potential risks that could impact their business. This includes conducting a thorough risk assessment to identify potential threats and vulnerabilities, as well as developing a risk management plan to address these risks. This might involve investing in insurance or taking steps to protect intellectual property, for example. By taking a proactive approach to risk management, entrepreneurs can reduce the likelihood of major disruptions to their business.

In 2020, with the onset of the COVID-19 pandemic, the travel industry was severely impacted, and Airbnb faced significant risks related to cancellations, refunds, and declines in bookings. To address these risks, Airbnb quickly implemented new policies and initiatives to protect hosts and guests, including allowing guests to cancel reservations without penalty, providing financial assistance to hosts who lost bookings, and implementing enhanced cleaning protocols.

In addition, Airbnb worked to diversify its business beyond just short-term rentals, launching new experiences and virtual options that were well-suited to the changing market conditions. By quickly identifying and mitigating risks, as well as adapting to new market conditions, Airbnb was able to weather the storm of the pandemic and remain a successful company.

Overcoming Obstacles and Challenges

Even the best-planned businesses will encounter obstacles and challenges along the way. Whether it's a sudden loss of revenue, a key employee leaving the company, or a legal dispute, entrepreneurs must be prepared to navigate these challenges with agility and resilience. This requires a combination of problem-solving skills, strong communication and leadership, and the ability to adapt to changing circumstances. By focusing on solutions rather than dwelling on problems, entrepreneurs can overcome challenges and keep their business moving forward.

Dealing with Failure and Pivoting When Necessary

Despite their best efforts, some entrepreneurs will experience failure at some point in their career. Whether it's a failed product launch or a business that never quite takes off, failure can be demoralizing and difficult to manage. However, successful entrepreneurs understand that failure is a natural part of the entrepreneurial process, and that it can be an opportunity for growth and learning. They also understand the importance of pivoting when necessary and may shift their business strategy in response to changing market conditions or other factors. By embracing failure and pivoting, when necessary, entrepreneurs can position themselves for long-term success.

An example of this can be seen with Instagram. Originally, the founders of Instagram created a social check-in app called Burbn, which allowed users to check-in at various locations and earn points. However, they found that users were mainly using the app to share photos, so they pivoted their focus to create a photo-sharing app instead.

After launching as a photo-sharing app, Instagram quickly gained popularity and attracted millions of users. However, the company faced another setback in 2012 when they released a new version of their app that received a lot of negative feedback from users. Instead of ignoring the feedback or doubling down on their original plan, Instagram quickly acknowledged the issues and released a new version of the app within days to address the problems.

By being willing to pivot and adapt to changing circumstances, Instagram was able to overcome setbacks and become one of the most popular social media platforms in the world.

Creating a Culture of Resilience

Managing risks and challenges requires more than just individual resilience - it also requires building a culture of resilience within the business. This means fostering a work environment where employees feel empowered to take risks, learn from failure, and adapt to change. It also means creating a supportive culture where team members are encouraged to speak openly and honestly about challenges and work together to find solutions.

Entrepreneurs can also take steps to build resilience in their business by investing in key areas such as technology, supply chain management, and employee training and development. By ensuring that their business is well-prepared to handle unexpected challenges, entrepreneurs can reduce the likelihood of disruptions that could impact their customers, employees, and bottom line.

Ultimately, managing risks and challenges is an ongoing process that requires constant attention and flexibility. By developing a proactive approach to risk management, embracing failure, and pivoting when necessary, and building a culture of resilience, entrepreneurs can position their businesses for long-term success in a rapidly changing business landscape.

Here are a few examples of companies that have developed a culture of resilience:

1. IBM: IBM is a company that has been around for over 100 years and has experienced its fair share of ups and downs. In the 1990s, the company went through a major restructuring, which led to significant job losses and

a decline in revenue. However, the company was able to bounce back by focusing on innovation and investing in emerging technologies.

2. Amazon: Amazon is a company that has experienced tremendous growth since its founding in 1994. However, the company has also faced a number of challenges along the way, including increased competition and regulatory scrutiny. Despite these challenges, Amazon has remained resilient by focusing on its customers, investing in new technologies, and constantly evolving its business model.

3. Netflix: Netflix is a company that has revolutionized the entertainment industry, but it has also faced its fair share of setbacks. In 2011, the company announced that it would be splitting its DVD rental and streaming services, which led to significant customer backlash and a decline in its stock price. However, the company was able to recover by quickly reversing its decision and refocusing on its core business of streaming.

These companies have all demonstrated the importance of building a culture of resilience, which has enabled them to overcome challenges and continue to grow and innovate.

In total, managing risks and challenges is a critical part of the entrepreneurial process. By taking a proactive approach to risk management, entrepreneurs can reduce the likelihood of major disruptions to their business. When facing obstacles and challenges, entrepreneurs must be prepared to navigate these challenges with agility and resilience, focusing on solutions rather than dwelling on problems. In the face of failure, entrepreneurs must embrace failure as a natural part of the process and pivot when necessary.

Remember, building a culture of resilience is an essential component of managing risks and challenges. This involves fostering a work environment where employees feel empowered to take risks, learn from failure, and adapt to change. It also means creating a supportive culture where team members are encouraged to speak openly and honestly about challenges and work together to find solutions.

With these strategies in mind, entrepreneurs can build businesses that are well-prepared to handle unexpected challenges and thrive in a dynamic business environment.

Chapter 8: Sustaining Success

"Sustaining success is not a one-time achievement, but a continuous journey of adaptation, innovation, and perseverance."

For entrepreneurs, achieving success is just the beginning. Sustaining success over the long-term requires ongoing effort and attention. In this chapter, we will explore and review some of the key strategies that entrepreneurs can use to sustain success and build businesses that stand the test of time.

Maintaining a Competitive Edge

To sustain success, entrepreneurs must maintain a competitive edge in their industry. This means staying up to date on market trends and evolving customer needs, as well as continuously innovating to stay ahead of the competition. Entrepreneurs must also focus on building a strong brand that resonates with their target audience and developing a reputation for quality and reliability.

A prime example of a company maintaining a competitive edge is Apple Inc.

Apple has maintained its competitive edge over the years through its innovative products, exceptional design, and excellent customer service. The company has been at the forefront of developing cutting-edge technology and constantly improving on its products to meet the changing needs of its customers.

Apple's competitive edge is also evident in its marketing strategy. The company's marketing campaigns are designed to create an emotional connection with its customers, and it has been successful in creating a strong brand loyalty among its customers.

Additionally, Apple's supply chain management is highly efficient, and the company has been able to minimize production costs and maximize profits through economies of scale. This has given the company a competitive advantage in the market, allowing it to offer high-quality products at a reasonable price while still maintaining profitability.

Innovating and Adapting to Changing Market Conditions

Another key strategy for sustaining success is the ability to innovate and adapt to changing market conditions. This requires a willingness to experiment and take calculated risks, as well as the ability to pivot quickly when new opportunities or challenges arise. Successful entrepreneurs must also be open to new ideas and perspectives, and willing to learn from their mistakes. Change is inevitable in business, but success lies in the ability to adapt and thrive in the face of it.

Building a Legacy and Giving Back to the Community

Finally, sustaining success is not just about building a profitable business - it's also about building a legacy and giving back to the community. Entrepreneurs can do this by focusing on creating a positive impact in the world, whether it's through charitable giving, environmental sustainability, or other social causes. By building a business that is not only financially successful but also socially responsible, entrepreneurs can create a legacy that extends beyond their own lifetime.

In the second half of this chapter, we will explore additional strategies for sustaining success, including cultivating strong partnerships, managing growth, and creating a culture of innovation and excellence.

here are a few examples of companies that have built a legacy and given back to the community:

1. TOMS: TOMS is a shoe company that has built a successful business model around giving back. For every pair of shoes purchased, TOMS donates a pair to a child in need. In addition to shoes, TOMS also donates eyewear and provides funding for clean water projects.

2. Patagonia: Patagonia is an outdoor clothing and gear company that has a strong commitment to environmental and social responsibility. The company has made significant efforts to reduce its environmental impact and has also donated millions of dollars to environmental causes.

3. Warby Parker: Warby Parker is an eyewear company that has a strong social mission. For every pair of glasses sold, the company donates a pair to someone in need. In addition, the company has worked to increase access to eye care services in underserved communities.

4. Ben & Jerry's: Ben & Jerry's is an ice cream company that has built its brand around social responsibility. The company has a strong commitment to using fair trade and non-GMO ingredients, and it also donates a portion of its profits to social and environmental causes.

5. Newman's Own: Newman's Own is a food company that was founded by actor Paul Newman. The company donates 100% of its profits to charity and has donated millions of dollars to a wide range of causes over the years.

Cultivating Strong Partnerships

Successful entrepreneurs understand that they can't do everything alone. Building strong partnerships with other businesses and organizations can help entrepreneurs leverage their strengths and expand their reach. By partnering with complementary businesses or organizations, entrepreneurs can access new markets, expand their product offerings, and benefit from shared resources and expertise.

Managing Growth

As mentioned previously, businesses grow, they face a whole new set of challenges. Entrepreneurs must be prepared to manage growth effectively, while still maintaining the quality of their products and services. This requires careful planning and attention to detail, as well as the ability to delegate responsibility and build a strong team.

Creating a Culture of Innovation and Excellence

This cannot be stressed enough, sustaining success requires creating a culture of innovation and excellence within the business. This means fostering a creative and collaborative work environment, where employees are encouraged to share ideas and take risks. It also means maintaining a strong focus on quality and customer satisfaction, and constantly seeking new ways to improve the business.

In this chapter, we have explored some of the key strategies that entrepreneurs can use to sustain success over the long-term. By maintaining a competitive edge, innovating, and adapting to changing market conditions, building a legacy and giving back to the community, cultivating strong partnerships, managing growth, and creating a culture of innovation and excellence, entrepreneurs can build businesses that stand the test of time.

Final Words

"Entrepreneurship is a journey where the destination is constantly shifting, but the experiences gained along the way are invaluable treasures that pave the path to success."

The entrepreneurial journey is a dynamic and challenging process, but it can also be incredibly rewarding and fulfilling. From generating ideas to sustaining success, entrepreneurs face a wide range of challenges and opportunities. However, with persistence, hard work, and a willingness to take risks, entrepreneurs can build successful businesses that make a difference in the world.

Throughout this book, we have explored the key steps involved in the entrepreneurial process, from generating ideas and conducting market research, to building a business plan, securing funding, and launching and growing the business. We have also discussed the risks and challenges that entrepreneurs face, and the strategies they can use to overcome these obstacles and sustain success over the long-term.

As you embark on your own entrepreneurial journey, we encourage you to take action and pursue your dreams. While the road may be challenging at times, the rewards can be significant, both personally and professionally. By following the steps outlined in this book, and by staying true to your vision and your values, you can build a business that has a positive impact on the world, and that brings you personal and financial fulfillment.

Remember that entrepreneurship is not just about making money, but about creating value for your customers and making a positive impact in your community. As you navigate the entrepreneurial journey, be sure to stay focused on your mission and your core values. Seek out the support and guidance of mentors, advisors, and other entrepreneurs who have walked this path before you. And above all, stay true to yourself and to your vision.

With the right mindset, skills, and resources, anyone can become an entrepreneur. Whether you are just starting out or are already well on your way, we hope that this book has provided you with the insights, tools, and inspiration you need to succeed. Remember that the entrepreneurial journey is a lifelong process of learning, growing, and evolving. Embrace the challenges and the opportunities that come your way, and never stop striving to be the best entrepreneur you can be.

It is my hope that after reading this handbook that you will think about how your ideas, talents, and drive can positively impact your community.

Read the story below and insert your name in the blanks.

[Reader's Name] was born and raised in a small town that had seen better days. As a child, they had watched businesses close one by one, leaving many families struggling to make ends meet. As they grew up, [Reader's Name] vowed to do something about it.

They decided to start their own business in the heart of their hometown. They worked tirelessly day and night, pouring all their passion and energy into creating a product that would not only be successful but also benefit the community.

Slowly but surely, word began to spread about [Reader's Name]'s business. More and more people started coming through the door, and the positive impact it was having on the local economy was undeniable. The business provided jobs to locals, partnered with other small businesses, and even hosted community events.

As the years went by, [Reader's Name]'s business grew beyond their wildest dreams, becoming a beloved institution in the town. But for [Reader's Name], it was never just about making money. It was about creating something that would last and make a difference in the community they loved.

[Reader's Name] felt an overwhelming sense of pride every time they walked down Main Street, seeing the vibrancy and life that had returned to their hometown. They knew that their business had played a small but important role in making that happen.

And it all started with a dream and a determination to make a positive impact. As [Reader's Name] reads this book, they feel inspired to take the first step towards making their own community a better place.

Always remember, Entrepreneurs are the dreamers, risk-takers, and doers who have the power to transform their visions into reality, and in doing so, they inspire others to follow in their footsteps. You are different for a reason. You were made to change the world.

Glossary of Terms

1. **Entrepreneurship:** The process of creating, developing, and growing a business venture with the goal of generating profits and adding value to society.

2. **Idea generation:** The process of brainstorming and identifying potential business concepts or opportunities.

3. **Market research:** The process of gathering and analyzing information about a particular market or industry to inform business decisions.

4. **Business plan:** A written document that outlines the key elements of a business, including the business model, marketing strategy, and financial projections.

5. **Funding:** The process of obtaining financial resources to support a business, including loans, grants, and investments.

6. **Launch:** The process of introducing a new business to the market and beginning operations.

7. **Scaling:** The process of growing and expanding a business to increase its reach and profitability.

8. **Risk management:** The process of identifying and mitigating potential risks to a business, including financial, legal, and operational risks.

9. **Innovation:** The process of developing new products, services, or business models that offer unique value to customers and give a business a competitive edge.

10. **Social responsibility:** The obligation of businesses to act in ways that benefit society and protect the environment, in addition to generating profits.

11. **Business model:** The way in which a company creates, delivers, and captures value for its customers, including its revenue streams, cost structure, and value proposition.

11. **Marketing strategy:** A plan for promoting and advertising a business, including market segmentation, targeting, and positioning.

12. **Cash flow:** The movement of money in and out of a business, including revenue, expenses, and investments.

13. **Pivot:** The process of changing the direction or strategy of a business to respond to changing market conditions or customer needs.

14. **Legacy:** The lasting impact of a business on its industry, community, and society.

15. **Competitive edge:** The unique advantage that a business has over its competitors, such as lower costs, better product quality, or superior customer service.

16. **Customer base:** The group of individuals or businesses that regularly buy products or services from a particular company.

17. **ROI:** Return on investment; a measure of the profitability of a business investment.

18. **Partnership:** A collaborative relationship between two or more businesses or individuals.

19. **Value proposition:** The unique value that a business offers to its customers, such as lower prices, better quality, or improved convenience.

Taking the first step to becoming the entrepreneur you were born to be. Believe me, I understand. But you do not have to go at it alone.

If you would like to learn more about starting your business or would like to have a conversation how to take your business to the next level, please email me below. I would love to have a chat.

About the Author

Mark E Lowe is a growth-oriented entrepreneur. He's personally launched six restaurants, and other side-hustles since 2003. He loves the challenge of getting all of the pieces in place at exactly the right time to ensure a successful launch. He is also a business consultant and the program chair for the Entrepreneurship program at Ivy Tech Community College, where he helps people launch their dream businesses. He is committed to lifelong learning. He holds earn a BS in psychology, an MA in experimental psychology, and an MS in human resources development. He currently resides in Lafayette Indiana with his wife, Annie.